IN HIS STRENGTH

ISBN 978-1-953194-88-6

ISBN 978-1-953194-14-5

Published by Believe In Your Books Publishing

Printed in the United States of America

For permission request, write to the publisher, addressed

"Attention: Permissions Coordinator" to the address below.

Email:BiybPublishing@gmail.com

Website: www.BelieveInYourBook.com

Table of Contents

IN HIS STRENGTH

"IN HIS STRENGTH, I PERSEVERED"

"IN HIS STRENGTH, I OVERCAME"

"IN HIS STRENGTH, I SURVIVED"

ACKNOWLEDGMENTS

Water is a symbol of purifying and cleaning, as I walk through the sand on the water of Sunny Isle Beach, I look up to heaven and communicate with my father, Abba. I come to my father as a humble servant with open arms praying while surrounded by many people, but in that moment it's just me and GOD. He then began to download information for me to write; speaking to his people. I'm writing TWO NOVELS at the same time which I'm only able to do this penmanship by the strength of GOD, I embrace being in his presence with great joy.

INTRODUCTION

This book was birthed at the beach on Monday morning, Memorial Day of 2016. I sat at the shoreline of the beach, looking up as my heavenly Father spoke to me, relaying a message to write to his people in great depth about actual encounters that happened to me and others throughout my life. The more I wrote, the more I cried as God showed me some life revelations. This book truly depicts the Word of God in Psalms 124:2: "If it wasn't for the Lord on my side, where would I be!" Throughout this book, God revealed how he has always been with me, even when I thought he was absent. He said, "I will never leave you nor forsake you."

In 1997, while driving home from the grocery store, I got into a bad car accident when an oncoming police patrol car t-boned my vehicle while I was making a left turn; the impact hit my car so hard that a standby vehicle was also hit. The accident involved three cars; the collision was so forceful that I was knocked unconscious. This was my second accident in two years. My vehicle encountered severe damage in the first accident, but no one was hurt. When I had awakened from being unconscious, I realized that I was lying on a stretcher and being put into the ambulance while articulating the 23rd Psalms. I could remember looking around at my surroundings, trying to figure out what had happened to me, in a distance, I noticed my husband was standing nearby holding our young son, who was crying and shaken up from the accident. As I think back, God could have taken me right then. I was asking God to help me as I was quoted the 23rd Psalms. I was a young wife and mother, not living a saved life at that time. "But oh, how my father, Abba, kept me in great strength and peace when I didn't know who or where I was". God allowed me to wake up speaking his word, line by line, as my physical body was in a state of confusion. Just think about it: how can someone unconscious wake up perfectly quoting a scripture? Only God can do that. I was operating in his strength and spirit. On that fateful night, God gave me another chance. MY GOD, MY GOD, TO BE KEPT BY YOU! I survived this accident with the prominent strength of my Father, Abba. GOD had my life in his hands, and I didn't realize it then. In the book of the Psalms, chapter 23, verse 4 states; Even though I walk through the [sunless] valley of the shadow of death. When I was unconscious, I was in that shadow of death, but My Father Abba was right there with me. He saw fit for me to wake up speaking his word, which is what he was speaking through me while I was unconscious. What an awesome God we serve. I am in complete awe of his presence. When this accident happened, I could not quite understand why I came back to consciousness quoting the 23rd Psalms, but now I have a unique understanding of why through the revelation of God's word. I was literally experiencing the omnipresence of God. This accident happened over nineteen years ago, and this revelation was revealed to me while writing this book. The second part of verse four of Psalms 23 states: I fear no evil, for you are with me; your rod [to protect] and your staff [to guide] comfort *and* console me. During my unconscious time, my Father Abba was doing this for me. His spirit was interceding on my behalf when I was in a state of senselessness, not knowing who or where I was. As I mentioned earlier, I was unconscious; however, this lasted an indefinite amount of time. But oh, to "Be Kept in His Strength" and not having a personal relationship with him before the accident was countless. I survived by the grace of the almighty God in an awful car accident in which the driver of one of the vehicles was hospitalized for days, and I was hospitalized for half a night for observations. With my Father's omnipotence, power, and strength, I overcame death staring me right in the face.

CHAPTER 1: ADULTERY

As I sat on the shoreline, thinking about how I would begin writing about this daunting experience, I became overwhelmed with tears. The night before I started writing my next chapter, God put on my heart to discuss adultery, but I was like, "God, I can't write about that; Lord, are you sure you want me to write about that?". I went to sleep that night thinking about how I would inscribe this story, hoping that God would give me something else to write about. The next day at work, during my morning break, God started speaking to me about writing about the adultery acts. Although I had been very hesitant and heavy in my spirit about writing on this matter, the Holy Spirit revealed to me what he wanted me to write about as I drove that day. I was worried about what my spouse might think or say, but God reminded me and said: "you are writing about your life, not his." The prophetic daily word also ministered to me as it stated, it is a valuable time to optimize your good traits and minimize your negative characteristics, says the Lord. This is all about being transformed, says the Lord; I am revealing many things that have been covered.

Romans 12:2

And do not be conformed to this world, but be transformed by the renewing of your mind, that ye may prove what that good, and acceptable and perfect, will of God is... Your mind

In the year 2000, as I was continuing my education at FIU North, working towards achieving my BA degree, I was a twenty-five-year-old wife and young mother now pregnant with my second child. Midway through my pregnancy, at my OBGYN appointment, the doctor noticed that my uterus was low, so he advised me that I could no longer be intimate until after the birth of my baby. I was in shock, to say the least, and really didn't know how my spouse would take it. But once I got home, I explained what the doctor told me, and he also had a surprised look. As months passed, I continued to attend college classes in the evening throughout the last trimester of my pregnancy term. Then, one faithful afternoon, my husband deliberately got into an argument with me so he can later leave and go out for the night.

Job 24:15

the eye of the adultery waits for the twilight, saying no eye will see me, and he covers his face.

People who commit adultery think that they are getting away from it because of the secretive way it is done. An adulterer is a detestable thing in God's eyes. My husband came home between the hours of 1 and 2 in the morning. He quickly took a shower and got into the bed to cuddle up behind me and rub my stomach. Later in that week, I heard a voice message from the doctor's office with information about my spouse's visit. When he came home from work, I inquired about this phone message, and he gave some lame excuse. A couple of weeks later, his conscience was bothering him, and as a result, he confessed to me that he cheated the night he stayed out. I was devastated, and my heart just dropped; I started fussing, cussing, and crying because here I was, eight and half months pregnant, and you go commit adultery. So, I began to take my wedding ring off and told him that I wanted a divorce. He then tries to console me and

Hebrews 13:4

marriage is to be held with honor and the marriage bed undefiled by immorality or sexual sin, for God will judge the sexually immoral and adulterous.

Within that same week, I took the clothes he had worn out that night and burned them out of anger. I was so furious, hurt, and frustrated that I had lost all trust.

I'm now thinking to myself, all because I had to stop being intimate to have his child. I became so bitter and irate that I wished that I could hurt him as much as I was hurting. The following weekend, my husband's phone rang very late in the night, so I answered it. The voice of a young lady was on the other end of the phone, and I became furious while conversing with her. I told her that he was a married man and to lose his number. She then informed me that he never said to her that he was married, and he was the one who pursued her. When my husband heard me on the phone, he was embarrassed because he never saw me in this manner. She never called him.

Proverbs 6:32

But a man who commits adultery has no sense; whoever does so destroy himself.

This kind of behavior destroys the person, and the family becomes devastated. The thought of another woman sitting in my husband's car while I was home eight months pregnant just infuriated me. During the last month of my pregnancy, I was emotionally and physically drained because all I did was cry. I was very depressed and hurt by my spouse's selfish behavior. The day my child was to be born, we had to go to the hospital early in the morning to

prepare for delivery. I was still having a hard time traveling in his vehicle; even though the seat was covered, I felt uncomfortable, betrayed, and dismayed. These feelings were constantly running through my mind. Later that evening, I gave birth to a healthy baby, and giving birth eased my pain a little. Then, fourteen-plus years later, I received a prophetic word for me to forgive my husband and the woman for the adultery act. I was so startled to hear this word because I was thinking to myself, "But I thought that I'd forgiven them", but apparently, I hadn't forgiven him or her; I just suppressed it.

Mathew 6:14

that if you forgive other people when they sin against you, your heavenly Father will also forgive you.

Therefore, writing about this situation has been so painful because I buried this hurt for all those years, and now, I'm crying, and my heart is very heavy as I write. I didn't want to report this chapter of my life, but God said I need you to be transformed. As I wrote about this situation. I cried, prayed, and cried. God revealed that my healing was taking place as I inscribed about this sensitive matter: I could not make it without him.

Revelation 12:11

they overcame because of the word of their testimony.

In his strength, I am obliged to write this chapter with heaviness in my heart and many tears, as God helped me to overcome a deep, hidden pain.

CHAPTER 2 : SURGERY

In July, before the birth of my child, difficult, unforeseen circumstances happened to Trudy. Trudy is a cousin who was in this medical situation. Due to these issues, she had to come to live with me because she was very ill; after her doctor's appointment, Trudy was told that she would need to have major surgery. Then, weeks later, I went to my last OBGYN appointment before I was to give birth, and during my appointment, I received a disturbing phone call. I was told that my godmother Charlie was at the hospital getting ready to have surgery. In route to the hospital, I had to begin to pray because so much was happening back-to-back with medical issues of different friends and family members.

> **Isaiah 41:10**
>
> **fear not, for I am with you, be not dismayed, for I am they God; I will strengthen thee.**

When I arrived at the hospital, family and friends were sitting in the waiting room, nervous and scared, not knowing what the outcome would be after the surgery. As we sat waiting patiently, everyone prayed individually for a successful surgery. The surgery took quite some time as we waited fearfully for the outcome. At the present time, I was nine months pregnant, sitting there scared and upset about my situation. The doctor told me at my appointment that if the baby did not come on its own in the next couple of days, then they would induce my labor. I was so upset to the point of crying because I just wanted the baby out of my stomach.

En route to the hospital, I was crying, stating, "I want this baby out of me." In Proverbs 16:9, Let me know that we may have our own plans, but God can change any plans because he establishes our steps according to his will for our life. Therefore, I was so upset about my own plans of when I should give birth. However, the Word of God teaches us that if we confide in him, there will be no room for hurt feelings or anger because God's timing is impeccable. I was mentally and physically exhausted with unforeseen circumstance going on with Trudy and Charlie, after several hours, the doctor finally came to the waiting area to update the condition after surgery. "To God Be the Glory." The surgery went well, and my loved one was now in the recovery room.

Isaiah 53:5

**5 But He was wounded for our transgressions,
He was crushed for our wickedness [our sin, our injustice, our wrongdoing];**

The punishment [required] for our well-being *fell* on Him,

And by His stripes (wounds), we are healed. The family was pleased and relieved that her body responded well to the surgery. A couple of days later, I went to the hospital early in the morning to have my delivery induced. I was thrilled to know that this was the day that I finally would get this baby out of my stomach. The following month, Trudy had her medical procedure done, which was only a month after I'd given birth. When she came home after surgery, I was still walking around tenderly and sore. I was put into a very untimely situation as I was caring for her and a newborn baby. Trudy was very weak, so I assisted her as well as my newborn. I started asking God for strength to handle these situations during this unfortunate time.

Psalms 31:24

24 Be of good courage, and he shall strengthen your heart, all ye that hope in the Lord.

It was indeed a lot for me to bear. I was a young wife who had just given birth to her second child, and my other family member was in the hospital recovering from a procedure. My God, My God, it was a journey for me in the latter months of the year. Through the two surgeries and delayed birth, I persevered in these difficult times. Still, I had to truly rely on God's strength because there was no way I could assist in my own strength.

Philippians 4:13

13 I can do all things [which He has called me to do] through Him who strengthens *and* empowers me [to fulfill His purpose—I am self-sufficient in Christ's sufficiency; I am ready for anything and equal to anything through Him who infuses me with inner strength and confident peace.]

I had to walk by this word during these unforeseen, strenuous times. In My Father's Abba strength, I overcame the surgery issues with my family and an overdue pregnancy that happened during a sensitive time in my marriage.

CHAPTER 3 : HOSPITAL

In 2005, as I was continuing my master's degree online at university, a medical situation hit my family hard. One evening, I got a call that Charlie was in ICU, and two days later, I got a call that my uncle Joseph just had a heart attack. In addition to the previous phone calls that same weekend, Turdy had a nervous breakdown. All three incidents happened within one week. Consequently, I had to constantly leave work early or just take the day off. When my supervisor realized it was too much for me, he advised me to take two weeks off to handle these family issues. While everything was happening so fast, I found myself in shock, walking around in a

dazed, trying to fathom all that had happened. I became worried about so much going on in my mind that I had to strive to not lose focus in my class assignments, as I would attempt to do some schoolwork in the waiting area of the different hospitals.

> **John 14:1**
>
> 14 "Do not let your heart be troubled (afraid, cowardly). Believe [confidently] in God *and* trust in Him, [have faith, hold on to it, rely on it, keep going, and] believe also in Me.

This situation became so overwhelming and stressful for me, to the point that I no longer had an appetite to eat. While driving all over town to three different hospitals, I began to ask God to strengthen me through this situation.

Psalms 73:26

When my flesh and heart is wounded and stretched out, God will strengthen me.

Charlie was located at a hospital in Dade. The family had been praying and praying over her because we literally almost lost her. Joseph was situated in a hospital in Broward. He had been suffering chest pains, which he thought were gas. But as the chest pains became more consistent, he then finally went to the hospital, where it was confirmed that he was indeed having a heart attack. He was put in ICU after a stint was put in his heart. During the weekend that all these events occurred Trudy had a big argument, which caused her to have a nervous breakdown.

Consequently, as the situation escalated between her and the other person, she became highly distraught that the authorities had to take her to the hospital. This situation put Trudy in a dark place, but God said otherwise.

Jeremiah 29:11

11 For I know the thoughts that I think toward you, saith the Lord, thoughts of peace, and not of evil, to give you an expected end.

I would drop my kids at school in the morning for two weeks and drive to the various hospitals to check on the family. I continued to pray for everyone's healing as I pressed my way through these unforeseen issues. I could return to work once everyone had gotten better and was released from the hospital. My supervisor asked me how I handled these difficult situations, and I said, "By the Grace of God." Throughout this stressful time in my life, I was not living a Christian life, but one thing I did know was how to pray and call on the name of Jesus! God was always with me, just like he said in his word.

Hebrews 13:5b

for He has said, "I will never [under any circumstances] desert you [nor give you up nor leave you without support, nor will I in any degree leave you helpless], nor will I forsake *or* let you down *or* relax My hold on you [assuredly not]!"

In his strength, I overcame the medical conditions that hit my family members simultaneously.

CHAPTER 4 : REPOSSESSION

In October 2011, I received a distressing call from one of my brothers who wanted to leave town, so I purchased a ticket for the Train. On Friday morning, I went and picked him up from his residence and took him to the train station. This unexpected situation caused me to move some bills around and get extensions for others. The following month, on Friday around midnight, I was awakened out of my sleep because I heard the truck alarm go off. So, when I looked out of the window, I noticed that my truck was missing; I then jumped out of bed and ran into the living room to see if my truck was indeed gone, and it was. I started pacing the floor, saying to myself, "Someone has stolen my truck", so I called the police. What I heard on the other end of the phone had me standing in a state of shock and embarrassment. The operator told me that my truck had not been stolen but was repossessed and that I would have to wait until Monday morning to contact the finance company. Due to the fact that the repossession took place over the weekend, there was no way I could have retrieved my vehicle. I began to cry, thinking, "I didn't realize that I was that far behind in my payments."

Job 1:21b

The Lord gave, and the Lord taken away; blessed be the name of the Lord.

My big sister Tiny called Saturday morning and asked if I was coming to church. Still, I told her about my transportation situation and that I couldn't make it. She later informed me that she would be coming to pick me up. I was feeling very heavy and didn't really want to go, but she was very adamant about coming to get me. I had a heaviness of heart during service, and at the end of the service, I got prayed for. In my distress, I had to meditate on the word of God.

Psalms 119:28

My soul is weary with sorrow; strengthen me according to your word.

When service ended, we went to the police station to see if we could get any information as to where the truck was located, but to no avail; they weren't of any help.

I came back home just as heavy as I was when I left because the police personnel were of no help to me. Sunday morning, my kids and I walked to the store, and they realized that the truck had been missing for a couple of days, so they began to ask me, "What happened to the truck, Mom?" too embarrassed to say what happened, I just told them that it was in the shop.

As I prepared for work on Sunday evening, I had to get mentally and physically ready to take public transportation from home to work. I was very aware of how the public transportation system worked because I've been catching the bus two to three times a week for ministry purposes, as I would pass out tracts to everyone I see; the meaning of tracts for me means *T- talking R-round A-about C-Christ T-teaches,* but during these times, I would park my truck at the train station and catch the public transportation voluntarily, now I find myself in a mandatory situation with no vehicle. Monday morning, as I walked to the bus stop, I felt very heavy in my spirit about my transportation situation. I really had to hold back my tears, but once I got to the bus stop, I talked to two young men about Christ and gave them some tracts; during my brokenness, God gave me the strength to still pass out tracts.

Philippians 4:6-7

6 Do not be anxious *or* worried about anything, but in everything [every circumstance and situation] by prayer and petition with thanksgiving, continue to make your [specific] requests known to God. 7 And the peace of God [that peace which reassures the heart, that peace] which transcends all understanding, [that peace which] stands guard over your hearts and your minds in Christ Jesus [is yours]. (A)reminds me to not be anxious or worried about anything, but in everything by prayer and petition with thanksgiving, continue to seek God in prayer.

At work, during my morning break, I went to the restroom and just started praying and crying out to God for favor before I made the call to the finance company. After praying, I called the finance company to determine how much money was needed to remove my truck from repossession. The lady on the phone told me that they usually wouldn't do this but that she would do this for me. She gave me all the information I needed, including where my vehicle was being held. When I got off the phone, I was overjoyed at how God had worked it out in my favor. Now I'm thinking to myself, I have all the information I need to retrieve my vehicle. Then I began to contemplate to myself, "How am I going to get this amount of money by the end of the week?" because my check wasn't quite enough. As I'm sitting and thinking about this in the locker room, then it was dropped in my spirit to ask my dad to assist me with some money towards the amount needed. I called my dad, crying while explaining everything because I never borrowed this money from him. This situation was very emotional for me. He advised me to stop crying and agreed to give me the money. Before I returned to my work area, I felt my strength returning as I could have all the funds needed to retrieve my truck. Friday couldn't come fast enough for me. I went on break, rushed to the bank to pay the appropriate amount, and received the receipt to go and pick up the truck from the pound. My vehicle had been repossessed for about a week, and those seven days were stressful and frustrating. My Father Abba gave me strength during this was wearisome as he gave me favors with the finance company and my dad. Approximately two weeks later, I was at my church with the homeless ministry. After we finished preparing the food to transport, we sat at the table in the office, and they began giving testimonies. I was sitting there listening to everyone give their testimony. Then the spirit of the Lord said to me, "Tell them what I did for you." Now I'm nervous and embarrassed cause I'm thinking to myself, I don't want them to know that my vehicle was repossessed; more testimonies were spoken. The Spirit of God spoke to me again and said, "Tell them what I did for you," so right before they were finishing up with testimonies, I finally obliged and I told my testimony of my repossessed vehicle and how God gave me the favor to retrieve my vehicle.

Revelation 12:11

they overcome by the Word of their testimony

So, my testimony helped blessed someone there to know that our God could do anything because nothing is too hard for him. Though I was heavy in my Spirit and embarrassed by my repossession, I persevered through the strength of my Father, Abba. He made a way out of nowhere for me to get my vehicle back.

CHAPTER 5 : BIOLOGICAL

In the early 90s, my life changed forever as I became a young mother at the tender age of eighteen while a freshman in college. Twelve years later, in February, devastating news struck me in my gut to the point that I felt like dying. This situation was so upsetting to me that I contemplated suicide. So many random thoughts ran through my mind while driving home from work every evening.

> **Psalms 13:3**
>
> **consider and answer me, O Lord my God; Give life to my eyes, or I will sleep the sleep of death.**

Most of the time, when people think this way, it is because they are seeking to escape the traumatic issues that they are facing at the present time. I had found out that the beautiful child I gave birth to as a freshman college student was not the biological child of my high school sweetheart, who was my husband at that time. This shattering and overwhelming news was very painful to me, as well as my marriage. I didn't know if I would be single or married at the end of the year. I was at work when I found out the news. I cried to my best friend, and she began to pray for me. For approximately two years, I would cry every day as I tried to remember what happened to me. During this time of heaviness, I would contemplate suicide.

Psalms 94:17-19

If the Lord had not been my help, I would soon have dwelt in the land of silence. If I say My foot has slipped, your compassion and lovingkindness, O Lord, will hold me up. When my anxious thoughts multiply within me, your comforts delight me.

During this time of my life, I was sporadically going to church off and on, but when this devastating issue hit my life, I began to pray more and more, seeking the face of God. I also started to go to church more often, like I did as a young child. In between considering suicide and remembering the Word of God that was taught to me, I felt like I was being pulled in two different directions. The more I thought about suicide, the more I pondered God's Word. This massive roadblock in my life put great tension on me emotionally and physically.

Psalms 6:6

I am weary with my groaning; every night I soak my bed with tears, I drench my couch with weeping.

In my prayer closet, I would continually ask God to help me remember what had happened to me. There were many days and months when just the thought of my situation would bring tears to my eyes. I would cry to sleep as I talked to God about understanding this storm.

me because he believed I deceived him. On the contrary, I could barely remember what had happened to me. I vaguely remember one very late night after work, I got a ride from a familiar face who was a friend of a family member. At the time of this ride, my high school boyfriend and I had broken up after dating for a couple of years, during which we were intimate. I remember being very tired from work and had a large cup of soda that I was drinking before leaving the building of my job. Unfortunately, on the ride home, I couldn't hardly remember what happened to me, but I recall saying, "Stop, stop!" During this time, I was being raped and didn't even realize it; I believe something was put into my drink because I was so drowsy that I could barely keep my eyes open. I was an eighteen-year-old senior in high school and had no clue what was happening to me.

2 Samuel 13:14

he would not listen to her, and since he was stronger than she, he violated her and lay with her.

Everything we go through in life is discussed in the Word of God, which helps us overcome trials and tribulations. God states in his Word that we will have trials and tribulations in this world, but be courageous, for he has overcome the world. Twelve years later, this unforeseen incident has now come to haunt me and traumatize my life. So, therefore, all these years, I think my child is from my high school sweetheart instead of from one scary night in which I was raped and didn't realize what happened to me. Consequently, I felt devastated and confused to find out the news about the biological issue of my child.

Psalms 9:9

he will be a refuge and a stronghold for the oppressed, a refuge in time of trouble.

Throughout this time, I kept seeking God for help, comfort, understanding, and, most importantly, peace of mind in the storm. My marriage was shaky as I continued telling my spouse what I remembered about the late-night encounter. Although I explained what had happened to me, he refused to believe or forgive me. So, for the next fourteen years, my marriage went on a roller coaster ride that ended up in the operation room. My spouse continued to be in an unforgivable state of mind but refused to divorce me. These were very strenuous times in my life and marriage. Amid this heavy weight on my shoulders, I started praying and reading my bible more than I had ever done in my life. I just wanted to be free of the pain and the guilt of not realizing what had happened to me on that fateful night. After two months of consistently seeking the face of God, I had an encounter that I will never forget. On this memorable night, I was asleep. I heard a small voice say to me, "I need your all," so I got up and looked at my husband, who was still snoring. I told myself that it wasn't him speaking. Then I laid back down, and a couple of minutes later, I heard it again, "I need your all." I then realized that it was the voice of the Lord. I started pleading with the Lord, saying, "I thought I was doing good, God. I go to church and sing in the choir". But what

I failed to realize is that I was a lukewarm Christian who was straddling the fence. Sometimes, I would do the church thing; sometimes, I wouldn't.

Revelation 3:15 -16

I know your deeds, that you are neither cold nor hot; I wish that you were cold or hot. So, because you are lukewarm, and neither hot nor cold, I will vomit you out of my mouth, meaning rejecting you with disgust.

God does not want his people to be lukewarm. He gives us a choice; we must try and make a conscious decision to be hot or cold. On this faithful night when God spoke to me, I started crying and crying as I began to say, "God, I would have been going to hell on a sliding board." God desires for you to surrender your all to him, not just part of you, but all of you, for he paid the ultimate price for us when he sent his son to die on the cross for our sins. Once I rededicated my life to Christ and surrendered my all to him, then and only then is when I able to release all the pain, heaviness, and sadness on him, for the Word of God teaches us to cast all our burdens on him, not some burdens but all our burdens for he cares for us. My relationship with God grew stronger and stronger every day. Months later, I was able to forgive myself for not understanding what had happened to me, as my healing process began with the love of God. I'm so glad that I surrendered my all to him. When you dedicate your life to God, there is no condemnation on you for your past.

Romans 8:1

therefore, there is now no condemnation (no guilty verdict, no punishment) for those who are in Christ Jesus (who believe in him as their personal Lord & Savior).

In April 2006, I joined a new Church and have been going forth in Jesus Christ as I surrendered my all to him. In Christ, I found my hope; in Christ, I found my joy; in Christ, I found my peace. During this great storm in my life, I survived. In his strength, I overcame this traumatic issue that shook my life upside down. In his strength, I survived those suicidal thoughts that were racing through my mind.

In his strength, I persevered when all odds were against me,

CHAPTER 6 : SPIRITUAL WARFARE

The Armor of God

Ephesians 6:12-17 Amplified Bible (AMP)

12 For our struggle is not against flesh and blood [contending only with physical opponents]. Still, against the rulers, against the powers, against the world forces of this [present] darkness, against the spiritual *forces* of wickedness in the heavenly (supernatural) *places*. 13 Therefore, put on the complete armor of God so that you will be able to [successfully] resist *and* stand your ground in the evil day [of danger], and having done everything [that the crisis demands], to stand firm [in your place, fully prepared, immovable, victorious]. 14 So stand firm *and* hold your ground, having [a]tightened the wide band of truth (personal integrity, moral courage) around your waist and having put on the breastplate of righteousness (an upright heart), 15 and having [b]strapped on your feet the gospel of peace in preparation [to face the enemy with firm-footed stability and the readiness produced by the good news]. 16 Above all, lift up the [protective] [c]shield of faith with which you can extinguish all the flaming arrows of the evil *one*. 17 And take the helmet of salvation, and the sword of the Spirit, which is the Word of God.

In dealing with Spiritual Warfare, you must be prepared by putting on the "Whole Armor of God," not part of the armor but the whole armor. We must put on six essential parts of the armor, which all work together. We need the other to wear one part. We need all parts to overcome and defeat the wiles of the enemy.

Also, we must continue to pray on all occasions without wavering. (1 Thessalonians 5:17-18)

Parts of the armor

- ❖ **BELT OF TRUTH**- the belt of truth involves our hearts and minds. This belt holds our armor in place. This is the first piece of the armor because we must know the truth. After all, Jesus is the way, the truth, and the light. (John 14:6)

- ❖ **BREASTPLATE OF RIGHTEOUSNESS**- the breastplate covers the upper parts of your chest area, where your heart, lungs, and other regions are. With this protective piece, you now become bold with confidence. Come boldly into his presence (Hebrews 4:16).

- ❖ **SHOES OF PEACE & PREPARATION** - the third piece of the armor allows us to step freely without fear while in battle. The Word of God states, "How beautiful are the feet of those who preach the gospel of peace." (Romans 10:15)

- ❖ **SHIELD OF FAITH**- this shield protects you from all the fiery darts of the evil one. The shield also protects our armor. In the battle, we must hold on to our profession of faith because he is faithful to do exactly what he said he would do. (Hebrews 10:23).

❖ **HELMET OF SALVATION - *the helmet*** is a crucial part of the armor. It protects our minds against all the lies that Satan tries to put in our minds because he wants us to doubt everything that God has told us. We must be serious and wear the armor of faith and love on our chests and a Helmet of Hope of Salvation. (1 Thessalonians 5:8)

❖ **SWORD OF THE SPIRIT** - the sword of the Spirit is the only weapon of the armor. Still, it is the best defense weapon because it is sharper than any two-edged sword that will cut to the marrow of the bones and discern the thoughts and intentions of the heart. (Hebrews 4:12)

CHAPTER 7 : SCHOLARSHIP

My godson, Joshua, graduated from high school as a State Football Champion with an undefeated season; although he had success during high school football, he was not highly recruited or, for better words, recruited at all. Out of the four or five colleges he applied to, the one college he desired the most was University CF, which did not accept him, and the University of SF College wanted to send him to their junior college. However, he did get an acceptance letter to start college in the summer of 2012 at a Local Florida University. Once he arrived at the college, he decided that he was going to be a walk-on for the football team.

The scholarship offers he got were mostly from small Junior colleges and a college in Florida. Something amazing happened to Joshua as he was moving into his dorm; a football coach came up to him and said, "Hey, I have been looking for you to get you fitted for your helmet." This situation just blew him away because Joshua's heart's desire was to go and try out for the football team as a walk-on player, but because of the favor of God, he didn't even know how to try out for the team; it seemed he had automatically been accepted as a walk on the player by the coaches. He was shocked because he had never tried out for the team, and they had already fitted him for his helmet.

Psalms 90:17

17 May the favor[a] of the Lord our God rest on us; establish the work of our hands for us— yes, establish the work of our hands. (A)

I thought it was strange and odd, but I gave God the Glory and informed Joshua that it was the favor of the Lord. I had been praying for years for Joshua to receive a football scholarship.

In his first walk-on season, he got hurt trying to do too much in tackling drills. Therefore, he had to redshirt his first season. During his time frame of recuperating and therapy, he began to get depressed and oppressed because he wanted to be out there to prove himself to the coaches so he could move up to the starting rotation and gain his scholarship. Therefore, I would continuously encourage Joshua to keep his head up, pray, and read His Word. In his second walk-on season, he began to strengthen with drills and work ethics but became frustrated that he was still with the scout team.

Galatians 6:9

9 Let us not grow weary *or* become discouraged in doing good, for at the proper time, we will reap if we do not give in.

As I continued to inform him to pray and trust God in his situation, I would have dreams that Joshua was getting close, but a wall was preventing him. I then began to realize that the wall was the work of the enemy blocking Joshua from moving forward in his college football career. I contacted my prayer partners to intercede with me as we began to fast and pray against the enemy's schemes.

Matthew 17:21

21 Howbeit this kind goeth not out but by prayer and fasting.

One evening, while riding the bus, I asked God why he had it so hard, and it seemed that his friends had it so easy. Then I heard the Holy Spirit say, "It's all the kingdom work you are doing." The enemy will attack your loved ones to take you off focus. Therefore, fasting and prayer are essential to defeat the enemy's wiles.

Early Sunday morning en route to church in September of 2014, the Spirit of the Lord said, "Scholarship." I just began worshipping, praising, and thanking God for what he was about to do. I later called Joshua and informed him of what thus saith the Lord and that God cannot lie if he said it, it must happen, because my bible tells me in

Numbers 23:19

"God is not a man, that He should lie,
Nor a son of man, that He should repent.
Has He said, and will He not do it?
Or has He spoken, and will He not make it good *and* fulfill it?

As the season was preparing to end, Joshua contemplated quitting because he had given one hundred percent effort in practice, and the scholarship players were giving sixty percent effort.

Despite what was happening around him on that football team, I would always give him scriptures to read. I had given him anointed oil to put on his body before every practice. The season ended, and still, no scholarship was awarded to Joshua, so he became very exasperated and contemplating quitting, but I kept encouraging, praying, and fasting and reminded him to stand on the Word of God because he couldn't lie; he said scholarship, and it shall come to past.

In the spring of 2016, the coach called him into the office early in the morning. Joshua went into that office nervously, not knowing what the coach wanted with him so early in the morning, but to his surprise, the coach told him that he appreciated all his hard work and dedication to the team, and for that, he has earned himself a *SCHOLARSHIP.* What a joy it was to hear that kind of news; when Joshua left the coach's office, he was shocked and overjoyed.

Then he called and gave me the news, and I cried while giving God all the Glory.

Isaiah 55:11

11 So will My Word be which goes out of My mouth; It will not return to Me void (useless, without result), Without accomplishing what I desire, and without succeeding *in the matter* for which I sent it.

He is faithful to his word; if he said it, that settles it, for he can't lie. Also, I reminded him of what God had said years before about his scholarship. He told his friends that he thanked God for his scholarship because, in the waiting process, he would always inform his football colleagues that he would get his scholarship. So, for the spring term of college football season, he could enjoy all the luxuries of being a scholarship player, with books being paid for and even a little check for personal expenses, things he could have never done while he was not on scholarship.

During this school term, he did not have to take out student loans, and what a blessing and relief for him, as he could get a refund check to save. Oh, what joy it was, from all the heartache, hard work, discouraging days, and oppressing times to just wanting to give up, but he preserved and stayed the course. This scholarship was awarded to him in the spring after the previous football season. When summer term began, he assumed his scholarship would roll over to the next semester. Still, unfortunately, it didn't, and it was just for that spring term. In the summer term, his last summer in college, he had to pay out of pocket, so there were more stressful days ahead as he prepared to play his final college football season, fighting for another scholarship.

Proverbs 3:5-6

5 Trust in *and* rely confidently on the Lord with all your heart

And do not rely on your own insight *or* **understanding.**

6 [a]**In all your ways know *and* acknowledge *and* recognize Him,**

And He will make your paths straight *and* smooth [removing obstacles that block your way].

As football camp started, Joshua became so irate and upset with how the coaches played him that he just about walked away. I began to war in the Spirit more with my prayer intercessors. I also kept encouraging him not to quit but to read the word and keep praying and seeking the face of God because God is not the author of confusion. I informed Joshua that if he said scholarship, he would bless you again. More scholarships were being given as football camp ended, and his name wasn't called. He then became more discouraged and prepared to quit his last football-eligible season. So, I continued to speak to him, encourage him not to be a quitter, and trust that God could do everything. I gave him more scriptures to read and study.

Philippians 4:13

13 I can do all things [which He has called me to do] through Him who strengthens *and* empowers me [to fulfill His purpose—I am self-sufficient in Christ's sufficiency; I am ready for anything and equal to anything through Him who infuses me with inner strength and confident peace.]

Now it seems all the scholarships were given out before the new season, "But God!" The next day, on Monday morning, Joshua was asked to go and see a coach, and what was said to him blew his mind. After hearing all the other players being awarded scholarships, he thought all was lost for him in his last season, but God showed up again.! The head coach told him that he appreciated his unselfishness in camp as they were playing all the younger players and not playing him, who was the more experienced player on the team. Also, he was commended for his cooperation and being a team player. He has rewarded him by awarding him another scholarship. My God is so unique; he did it again. Joshua was blessed with a double blessing.

A scholarship, when all the odds were against him being on the scout team for three years of college football. Though the walking journey was rough and tough, he overcame all the adversity with the strength of God. We preserved through much praying, fasting, and intercessors. God did exactly what he said he would do: Scholarship, Scholarship, and Scholarship to God Be the Glory!!!

CHAPTER 8 : CEREMONY

In February of 2016, the Spirit of the Lord spoke to me about my ceremony; he said, "It's going to be hard, but he is right with me; I'm the only one who can stop the progress; I have to continue to plan the ceremony." So, in March of 2016, I went by faith with my best friend to the hall that God had ordained and shown me in a dream and put down five hundred dollars to hold my spot for my 20th-anniversary ceremony, which I was so nervous about. Still, I kept trusting in what God had spoken to me last month. In the latter part of March of 2015, my husband and I went on our nineteenth-anniversary trip to DM. We had a wonderful time traveling internationally for the first time. During the trip, I kept mentioning to my spouse that we would have a renewal of vows ceremony for our 20th anniversary. At times, my husband would agree and other times, he would disagree because of too much money. In the past couple of years, we have been to two weddings. One of the weddings was of a family member, and the other was of a neighbor we barely knew. My spouse has a passion for married people, so he was very excited to go to the wedding of our neighbor, whom we had known for less than a year. Months later, after the wedding, there was a discussion between the neighbor and my husband, in which my husband stated, "I never had a big wedding."

Therefore, deep in my spouse's heart, he desired the wedding we never had because we were married very young with limited finances. In 1997, we got married at the courthouse, and on our honeymoon, we went to the Bahamas with our three-year-old son. So, we never had a wedding ceremony where friends and the family could come and celebrate with us. After having a great time on our 19th-anniversary trip, things changed drastically in our marriage once we came home.

On the latter days of the month, my husband watched a strange video with his back turned; at the time, I did not know what he was watching. That night, I had a dream, and in the dream, I was at the ATM machine, and on my receipt, it stated, "That is a spirit," and I was like My God. I woke up from the dream mad and furious with the enemy. So, I immediately contacted my prayer warriors to pray and intercede for my marriage.

2 CORINTHIANS 10:3-5

3 For though we walk in the flesh [as mortal men], we are not carrying on our [spiritual] warfare according to flesh *and* using man's weapons. 4 The weapons of our warfare are not physical [weapons of flesh and blood]. Our weapons are divinely powerful for the destruction of fortresses. 5 *We are* destroying sophisticated arguments and every exalted *and* proud thing that sets itself up against the [true] knowledge of God, and *we are* taking every thought *and* purpose captive to the obedience of Christ,

Afterward, I started praying throughout my house, warring in the Spirit, speaking in my heavenly language, and walking throughout every room; then I proceeded outside my house to walk around my house, anointing every place as I walked with the whole armor on and repeated the Word of God in **Joshua 24:15, "As for me and my house we will serve the Lord."**

I pleaded the blood over my house, over my kids, over me, and continued to pray that the defiled Spirit lose my husband. After I finished praying throughout my house, one of my prayer partners called with a prophetic word from the Lord. The Spirit of the Lord said, "he will never leave nor forsake me; fear not, for I am with you. You have chosen to serve the Lord in your house, standing for righteousness in thy nation, and he is sending an archangel, Michael, to my household because you, my daughter, want to renew your vows. The enemy is fighting against unity and marriages because you have a story you must go through to show other women who are willing to fight for their marriages that it can be done!". The word of God states an unbelieving husband is sanctified through his wife. (1 Corinthians 7:14) The enemy has my husband thinking he is God and worship the light, there were a dark covering over his eye gates and ear gates, so therefore he can't receive any positive word about who God is. The enemy had blinded him to the point that he screamed at me and our child, stating, "I will not read the bible!" All this spiritual warfare started taking place after we came back from our anniversary trip, and I later realized that the enemy was mad at me for stepping out of faith in planning the 20th-anniversary ceremony. The devil hates unity, so he would do anything to bring discord and division into a household. In this spiritual warfare, I was fasting for months, praying multiple times daily, continually reading the word on deliverance and understanding what types of spirits was I dealing with? My prayer life had to change drastically, and I had to read and quote those scriptures during prayer. God's word is the only weapon of the armor; it is sharper than a two-edged sword that cuts the marrow of the bones.

During this challenging time, God told me to continue to plan the ceremony because it is ordained, and couples that attend will be blessed. April was tough, but I kept pressing, praying, fasting, and studying the Word of God. During February to March of the following year, I was in spiritual warfare for my ceremony; it was a year of straight warfare.

EPHESIANS 6:11-17

11 Put on the full armor of God [for His precepts are like the splendid armor of a heavily armed soldier], so that you may be able to [successfully] stand up against all the schemes *and* the strategies *and* the deceits of the devil. 12 For our struggle is not against flesh and blood [contending only with physical opponents], but against the rulers, against the powers, against the world forces of this [present] darkness, against the spiritual *forces* of wickedness in the heavenly (supernatural) *places*. 13 Therefore, put on the complete armor of God so that you will be able to [successfully] resist *and* stand your ground in the evil day [of danger], and having done everything [that the crisis demands], to stand firm [in your place, fully prepared, immovable, victorious]. 14 So stand firm *and* hold your ground, having [a] tightened the wide band of truth (personal integrity, moral courage) around your waist and having put on the breastplate of righteousness (an upright heart), 15 and having [b] strapped on your feet the gospel of peace in preparation [to face the enemy with firm-footed stability and the readiness produced by the good news]. 16 Above all, lift up the [protective] [c] shield of faith with which you can extinguish all the flaming arrows of the evil *one*. 17 And take the helmet of salvation, and the sword of the Spirit, which is the Word of God.

I had lost so much weight from continually fasting and did not have an appetite to eat when I was not fasting. I was on a twenty-one-day fast while in spiritual warfare for my ceremony. During this period, I drove home every day from work with a heavy weight on my shoulders.

No matter how much I prayed with my prayer partners at work, I still drove home with heaviness after work every day while making all the plans for the ceremony.

EXODUS 14:14

14 The Lord will fight for you while you [only need to] keep silent *and* remain calm."

There was no emotional or financial support from my spouse; it was just God and me the whole time; he directed my path in the process. The stress on me was later put on the kids because my husband kept telling them that he would not show up and that I was wasting my time and money planning the ceremony.

PROVERBS 3:5-6

5 Trust in the Lord with all your heart and lean not on your own understanding; 6 in all your ways submit to him, and he will make your paths straight.[a]

Therefore, I had to continually pray over my kids and anoint them. I would tell them, "God doesn't lie. If God told me to continue to plan the ceremony, then that's what I'm going to do". I told my kids to follow me as I follow God. En route to work, as my 21-day fasting was ending, the Spirit of the Lord started ministering to me in August. The Lord said, "Your husband will apologize to you for his behavior, your labor will not go in vain, and you will teach other people how to stand on the battlefield and not waver by praying, fasting, and reading the Word of God saith the Lord." During my 21 days journey, my planning had been put to a halt, so this morning, while God was speaking to me, I asked God if I could continue planning this ceremony, and the Lord said, "You Shall Pursue." as the Lord spoke these words to me, I cried, cried, and cried. Months later, I went to get fitted for my dress. Still, during this time frame, I was very heavy in my Spirit from all the negative speaking and behavior from my husband, as I continued to purchase all the necessities to have a beautiful ceremony.

Almost about a day out of every week, my spouse would continuously say, "I'm not coming to the ceremony; you are wasting your money." yes, his actions kept me heavy in my Spirit, but I would take everything he said to the Lord in prayer.

Philippians 4:6-8

6 Do not be anxious about anything,(A) but in every situation, by prayer and petition, with thanksgiving, present your requests to God. (B) 7 And the peace of God,(C) which transcends all understanding,(D) will guard your hearts and your minds in Christ Jesus.
8 Finally, brothers and sisters, whatever is true, whatever is noble, whatever is right, whatever is pure, whatever is lovely, whatever is admirable—if anything is excellent or praiseworthy—think about such things.

Once all the invitations were sent out, my neighbor came to my husband to say congratulations; he told the neighbor that he was not going, so don't show up. He later spoke to his father and told him the same thing: not coming down to attend the event because he was not going.

I kept experiencing all this negative behavior from my husband, all the while planning a beautiful, unique twentieth-anniversary ceremony for us, not just for me, but for us.

John 10:10

10 The thief cometh not, but for to steal, and to kill, and to destroy: I am come that they might have life, and that they might have it more abundantly.

The stronghold on his mind was real, and he didn't even realize how damaging it was to his soul, family, and friends.

2 Corinthians 10:5

5 We demolish arguments and every pretension that sets itself up against the knowledge of God,(A) and we take captive every thought to make it obedient(B) to Christ.

A couple of weeks before my special ceremony, our children were stressed and overwhelmed because of all the negativity their dad would say about the ceremony. Still, I had to assure them not to worry about what he said and just follow me as I follow God. Then, my spouse went to the extreme to tell our son to take his suit back, which he had rented. I had to intervene and explain to my kids that what their dad was saying was a spirit operating in him, but trust God because God can't lie, and if he said it, it should come to pass.

Psalm 33:20-21

20 We wait [expectantly] for the Lord;
He is our help and our shield.
21 For in Him our heart rejoices,
Because we trust [lean on, rely on, and are confident] in His holy name.

Before the ceremony, I imagined myself walking down the aisle. Still, all I could see were my husband's shoes. From the shoes, I realized that not only was he going to show up, but he was going to wear something from his closet because he refused to rent a tuxedo. Twenty-four hours before the ceremony, my husband was sending negative texts, saying he was not coming and that I was turning our children against him.

Psalm 21:11

11 For they planned evil against You;
They devised a [malevolent] plot
And they will not succeed

The enemy fought me so hard all the way to the day of my ceremony that he was trying to make me give up. Still, I kept praying, fasting, and trusting God wholeheartedly. In March of 2017, the day of my ceremony, my MC called me and said, "For the record, the groom is here." I started screaming, saying, "Look at God, look at God, God doesn't lie," and my child's mouth dropped wide open. She was just in shock, and I began to praise God in tears and speak in my heavenly language because God can't lie. I had to continue to trust him even when it didn't feel good or look good with a heavy heart twenty-four hours before the ceremony. I went through fourteen months of spiritual warfare for my ordained 20th-year renewal of vows ceremony; what a journey this was, but God! I had to truly rely on God's strength as I endured fiery dots from the enemy for over a year during my planning. I persevered when all odds were against me in dealing with my husband, who was impressed and enjoyed the beautiful ceremony. This situation was one of the most challenging times in my marriage, all because I desired to renew my vows with a wedding that we never had nineteen years ago. The enemy attacked me through my husband, who is not saved, but God doesn't lose battles; if he says you shall pursue, then pursue because he has your back!

SPIRITUAL WARFARE IS REAL. You need the whole armor of God, the Word, and the Holy Ghost to defeat the enemy's wiles. With God, I overcame all the demonic attacks against me as I planned our ceremony. In his strength, I persevered, overcame, and survived!

CHAPTER 9 : IDENTITY

In the latter month of the year, my cousin Abby called me after she came home from school, and she sounded exhausted and overwhelmed. I started asking her all kinds of questions, "Did someone do something to you or say something to you out of the way?" but she kept telling me no. Afterward, she said she didn't know how to tell me but had a long day. So, after much questioning, she told me to call her teacher, and he would explain what happened in school that day. I became very nervous and upset and proceeded to call the teacher and speak to him, and what he told me had me speechless and angry. Once I got off the phone, I went to visit Abby to have a talk with her. When I began to question her about how long she had been feeling or thinking this way, she told me that at a very young age, the enemy had been making her believe that she was bisexual. I began to rebuke the enemy and say, "The devil is a liar," and that she is marvelous and wonderfully made in the image of God, a young girl who likes boys.

Psalm 139:13-14

13 For You formed my innermost parts;
You knit me [together] in my mother's womb.
14 I will give thanks *and* praise to You, for I am fearfully and
wonderfully made;

Wonderful are Your works, And my soul knows it very well.

On Friday evening, my church had a corporate prayer. So, later that evening, I got dressed and went and picked up Abby, and then we proceeded to church for prayer. En route to church, I began to war in the Spirit for her soul, mind, and body; as she repeated the Word of God after me, she and I began to cry out loud to the Lord. For the next couple of months, I began to teach and show Abby the Word of God against that nasty Spirit, and I reminded her that God is not the author of confusion. That is the work of the enemy.

Leviticus 18:22, 20:13

22 "Do not have sexual relations with a man as one does with a woman; that is detestable.
13 If a man also lies with mankind, as he lieth with a woman, both of them have committed an abomination: they shall surely be put to death; their blood shall be upon them.

I told her to write down the Word of God and read it every night and day. Also, she took them to school with her. Every day, I would call her to see where her mind was and inquire if the enemy was still confusing her about her identity. She told me that the enemy would confuse her mind as soon she got on the school bus. I went into warfare for Abby and started to plead the Blood of Jesus over her mind. It came to a point at school where the kids began falsely accusing her, but she took out the Word of God that she had written on index cards and began to show those students what God said about that homosexual Spirit and that God did not make us like that; then the kids backed off her and stopped teasing her. During this challenging time, I began fasting and praying, seeking the face of the Lord and binding that Spirit off her.

James 4:7

7 Submit yourselves, therefore, to God. Resist the devil, and he will flee from you.

About a month later, the Spirit of the Lord told me to build an altar and pray for her every night and morning. I denounce, renounce, and rebuke every defiled Spirit that tries to confuse Abby about her identity. While in prayer, the Spirit of the Lord told me to have her get rid of

some clothes to which that defile spirit was attached. Nevertheless, I continued in spiritual warfare for her, as I taught her to repeat this scripture, *"As for me and my house we will serve the Lord." (Joshua 24:15).* In the latter weeks of the end of the year, I began to speak and meditate on that word with Abby, and we have never look back. This scripture has become my anthem in prayer. At the beginning of the new year, Abby got a beautiful hairstyle and started to realize how beautiful she was. Where the enemy had tried to confuse her mind, God wanted her to know that she was a gorgeous young lady marvelously made in his image.

1 Corinthians 14:33

33 For God is not the author of confusion, but of peace, as in all churches of the saints.

She returned to school with a new and improved look, where some classmates did not even recognize her. Young men were trying to talk to her. When all this began, Abby's confidence grew as she finally embraced her beauty. So many kids at her school were battling with that Spirit, so they should not have taken prayer out of the schools. We must continue to pray daily for our family, friends, and the world.

1 Thessalonians 5:17

17 be unceasing *and* persistent in prayer.

I also informed her that the enemy is trying to stop what God has created from the beginning, male & female, together to procreate.

1 Peter 5:8

8 Be alert and of sober mind. Your enemy, the devil, prowls around like a roaring lion, looking for someone to devour.

It was very upsetting for me to find out that Abby had been battling her identity for over five years. I constantly encouraged and uplifted her, telling her she was a gorgeous young lady. Later in the year, she went to an event and wore make-up for the first time; she was so beautiful that she couldn't believe it was her in the mirror looking gorgeous. Afterward, I continually prayed for her because the enemy comes to steal, destroy, and test your faith to see if you are delivered. However, a few months later, I started to discern that Spirit was trying to linger around Abby. So, every day for about three weeks, I would call and inquire to see if the enemy was speaking to her mind or trying to confuse her about her identity. Still, she would always say "NO," and she started to get frustrated with me. I just couldn't shake this feeling, so I kept calling and asking her every other day.

2 Corinthians 10:3-5

3 For though we live in the world, we do not wage war as the world does. 4 The weapons we fight with are not the weapons of the world. On the contrary, they have divine power to demolish strongholds. 5 We demolish arguments and every pretension that sets itself up against the knowledge of God, and we take captive every thought to make it obedient to Christ.

Then, I began to war with the spirit speaking in my heavenly language in my prayer closet. One night, I had a demonic attack in my dream, which showed me the spirit that I was feeling was there trying to be a doormat around Abby. Still, I thank God for the Holy Ghost, who allowed me to discern the spirit that was trying to linger around.

Ephesians 6:11

11 Put on the full armor of God [for His precepts are like the splendid armor of a heavily armed soldier], so that you may be able to [successfully] stand up against all the schemes *and* the strategies *and* the deceits of the devil.

In my dream, I was praying for Abby as I've always done, and after praying, I saw the demonic spirit jump up and come running towards me, saying "nooo," and trying to attack me.

I grabbed the spirit by the throat and kept speaking in my heavenly language and pleading for the blood of Jesus; I said, "You are kind of strong, but my God is stronger." I went into warring with that spirit until it left. In spiritual warfare, you must be prepared for battle dressed in the Whole Armor to defeat the enemy. Put on the full armor of God so that you can take your stand against

Ephesians 6:13-17

13 Therefore, put on the complete armor of God, so that you will be able to [successfully] resist *and* stand your ground in the evil day [of danger], and having done everything [that the crisis demands], to stand firm [in your place, fully prepared, immovable, victorious]. 14 So stand firm *and* hold your ground, having [a]tightened the wide band of truth (personal integrity, moral courage) around your waist and having put on the breastplate of righteousness (an upright heart), 15 and having [b]strapped on your feet the gospel of peace in preparation [to face the enemy with firm-footed stability and the readiness produced by the good news]. 16 Above all, lift up the [protective] [c]shield of faith with which you can extinguish all the flaming arrows of the evil *one*. 17 And take the helmet of salvation, and the sword of the Spirit, which is the Word of God.

This situation took many months, days, and hours, reading the word, praying, and fasting. Some circumstances only change through fasting and prayer.

Matthew 17:21

21 [a] [But this kind of demon does not go out except by prayer and fasting.]"

Prayer is mighty; fasting and praying are the best weapons against spiritual forces. Throughout the years of praying with and for Abby, I thank God for the power he gives us to conquer the enemy; in his strength, we overcame the enemy's wiles that tried to confuse her about her identity.

Luke 10:19

Behold! I have given you authority *and* power to trample upon serpents and scorpions and physical and mental strength and ability over all the power that the enemy [possesses], and nothing shall in any way harm you.

CHAPTER 10 CONCLUSION

<u>PSALMS 25:7-8</u>

7 The Lord is my strength and my shield;

my heart trusts in him, and he helps me.

My heart leaps for joy,

and with my song, I praise him.

8 The Lord is the strength of his people,

a fortress of salvation for his anointed one

As I conclude, I've shared some difficult situations in which I persevered through these obstacles on the strength of my Lord and Savior. I am honored that God gave this book out of me, which encourages and motivates his people. God loves us so much that it is so amazing and unexplainable.

> **2 Peter 3:9**
>
> **9 The Lord is not slow in keeping his promise, as some understand slowness. Instead, he is patient with you, not wanting anyone to perish, but everyone to come to repentance.**

My challenging circumstances represent many people worldwide who have gone through similar situations. In this book, God shows and teaches his people how to trust him in every situation we go through. No matter how hard or uncomfortable it may be, he always desires us to trust him.

If you don't have a personal relationship with God, now is the time to seek his face and open your heart to receive him, for he sees all and knows all.

ROMANS 10:9-10

9 because if you acknowledge and confess with your mouth that Jesus is Lord [recognizing His power, authority, and majesty as God], and believe in your heart that God raised Him from the dead, you will be saved. 10 For with the heart a person believes [in Christ as Savior] resulting in his justification [that is, being made righteous—being freed of the guilt of sin and made acceptable to God]; and with the mouth he acknowledges and confesses [his faith openly], resulting in and confirming [his] salvation.

As you surrender your life to God, you will see his hand move over all your circumstances. Trust in the Lord, and don't try to handle your problems on your own because you will fail every time.

Proverbs 3:6

6 [In all your ways know *and* acknowledge *and* recognize Him,

And He will make your paths straight **and** **smooth [removing obstacles that block your way].**

This means in every condition, every problem, every trial, in all your ways, not some issues, but all your problems, and he shall direct your paths.

www.ingramcontent.com/pod-product-compliance
Lightning Source LLC
Chambersburg PA
CBHW061324120626
46546CB00007B/2670